W9-BXU-350

Cool
CREEPY
FOOD ART

Easy Recipes That Make Food Fun to Eat!

Nancy Tuminelly

ABDO
Publishing Company

To Adult Helpers

This is not your ordinary cookbook! Sure, we've provided ingredients lists and how-to photographs. But like any artistic endeavor, food art is all about creativity! Encourage kids to come up with their own ideas. Get creative with ingredients too. Scan your fridge and get started with whatever you have!

Always supervise kids when they are working in the kitchen. Food art often requires a lot of knife work such as slicing and shaping. Assist young artists whenever they are using knives. Occasionally, kids will need to use the oven or stovetop too. Be there to help when necessary, but encourage them to do as much as they can on their own. Kids love to share and eat their own creations!

Expect your young food artists to make a mess, but also expect them to clean up after themselves. Show them how to properly store unused ingredients. Most importantly, be a voice of encouragement. You might even get kids to eat healthy foods they've never had before!

Visit us at www.abdopublishing.com

Published by ABDO Publishing Company, 8000 West 78th Street, Edina, Minnesota 55439. Copyright © 2011 by Abdo Consulting Group, Inc. International copyrights reserved in all countries. No part of this book may be reproduced in any form without written permission from the publisher. Checkerboard Library™ is a trademark and logo of ABDO Publishing Company.

Printed in the United States of America, North Mankato, Minnesota
062010
092010

 PRINTED ON RECYCLED PAPER

Editor: Liz Salzmann
Series Concept: Nancy Tuminelly
Cover and Interior Design: Anders Hanson, Mighty Media, Inc.
Photo Credits: Anders Hanson, Shutterstock

The following manufacturers/names appearing in this book are trademarks:
7-Up®, Archer Farms®, Indian Summer®, Jell-o®, Market Pantry®, Morton®, Ragú®, ReaLemon®, Tostitos®

Library of Congress Cataloging-in-Publication Data

Tuminelly, Nancy, 1952-
  Cool creepy food art : easy recipes that make food fun to eat! / Nancy Tuminelly.
      p. cm. -- (Cool food art)
  Includes index.
   ISBN 978-1-61613-363-4
  1. Cookery--Juvenile literature. 2. Food presentation--Juvenile literature. I. Title.
  TX652.5.T837 2011
  641.5--dc22
                            2010003286

CONTENTS

PAGE 16

Play with Your Food!   4

The Basics   5

The Coolest Ingredients   8

The Tool Box   10

Cooking Terms   11

Techniques   12

Severed Finger Pizza   **14**

Floating Head Cider   **16**

To Die For Dip   **18**

Eyeball Spaghetti   **20**

Gross-out Pita   **22**

Garbage Goop   **24**

Bloody Hand Punch   **26**

Snot Stick Pretzels   **28**

Wrap It Up!   30

Glossary   31

Web Sites   31

Index   32

PAGE 18

PAGE 24

PAGE 26

PLAY WITH YOUR FOOD!

Unless Mom says not to!

It's time to play with your food! Get ready to make floating heads, severed fingers, and eyeball spaghetti! You're an artist now. The plate is your **canvas**, and your favorite foods are your paints!

As you make your creepy food art, be open to all sorts of ingredients. You can use anything! Fresh fruits and vegetables work great. You can shape and slice them in so many ways!

Use foods that you like, but don't be afraid to try new things.

Like any kind of art, food art is about **expression** and creativity. Get inspired and give each dish your own special touch. A lot of cookbooks teach you how to make food that tastes great. This book will inspire you to make creepy foods that taste and look great!

THE BASICS

Get started with a few important basics

ASK PERMISSION

➤ Before you cook, get permission to use the kitchen, cooking tools, and ingredients.

➤ You might want an adult to help you with some of your creations. But if you want to do something yourself, say so!

➤ When you need help, just ask. An adult should always be around when you are using sharp knives, the oven, or the stove.

BE PREPARED

➤ Read through the recipe before you begin.

➤ Get organized. Have your tools and ingredients ready before you start.

➤ Think of **alternative** ingredients if you want!

BE SMART, BE SAFE

> Never work in the kitchen when you are home alone!

> Have an adult nearby when you are using sharp tools such as a knife, peeler, or grater. Always use sharp tools with care. Use a cutting board when you are working with a knife.

> Work slowly and carefully. Great food art rarely happens when you rush!

BE NEAT AND CLEAN

> Start with clean hands, clean tools, and a clean work surface.

> Always wash fruits and vegetables. Rinse them under cold water. Pat them dry with a towel. Then they won't slip when you cut them.

> Tie back long hair so it stays out of the way and out of the food!

> Wear comfortable clothes that can get a little bit dirty. Roll up your sleeves.

Note on Measuring

The recipes in this book provide **approximations**. Feel free to be creative! For example, a recipe may call for 1 tablespoon of cream cheese. Do you like cream cheese? Then add more! If you don't like cream cheese, then try something else!

SHOPPING FOR PRODUCE

Sometimes canned produce works perfectly in your food art. But more often than not, fresh fruits and vegetables are better. When you are shopping for your food art groceries, think about what you are making. For example, do you want a really big carrot or a small one? Fruits and vegetables come in all different shapes and sizes! Think about the shapes and sizes that will work best in your food art.

SAVING INGREDIENTS

When you are making food art, sometimes you only need a little bit of something. That means you have to do a good job of putting things away so they stay fresh. Cover leftover ingredients so that they will keep. Airtight containers work best. You don't want to waste a lot of food!

KEY SYMBOLS

In this book, you will see some symbols beside the recipes. Here is what they mean.

Sharp!

You need to use a knife for this recipe. Ask an adult to stand by.

Hot!

This activity requires the use of an oven or stove. You need adult supervision. Always use oven mitts when holding hot pans.

THE COOLEST

STRING CHEESE

SHREDDED CHEDDAR CHEESE

SHREDDED MOZZARELLA CHEESE

SLICED MOZZARELLA CHEESE

CHEESE DIP

SPAGHETTI NOODLES

7-INCH PIZZA CRUST

SMALL PITA POCKETS

LARGE PRETZEL STICKS

ALMOND SLICES

SALT

PICKLE RELISH

PIZZA SAUCE

PASTA SAUCE

SALSA

GUMMY WORMS

FRUIT LEATHER ROLLS

PULL AND PEEL LICORICE

GUMMY BUGS

INGREDIENTS

GREEN OLIVES
WITH PIMIENTO

BLACK OLIVES

BELL PEPPERS

LETTUCE

CAULIFLOWER
HEAD

CARROTS

GRAPE
TOMATOES

GRANNY SMITH
APPLE

RASPBERRIES

RAISINS

LEMON JUICE

APPLE JUICE

APPLE CIDER

CRANBERRY JUICE

7-UP

GELATIN
DESSERT MIX

FOOD COLORING

FROZEN
MEATBALLS

THE TOOL BOX

Here are some tools you'll need for most food art recipes

PARING KNIFE

APPLE CORER

PEELER

KITCHEN SCISSORS

SPATULA

BAKING SHEET

STRAINER

CUTTING BOARD

SAUCE PAN

LADLE

MEASURING CUPS
AND SPOONS

6-OUNCE CLEAR JARS

STEW POT

MIXING BOWLS

PARCHMENT PAPER

PREP BOWLS

TOOTHPICKS

COOKING TERMS

A simple list of words you'll want to know

CHOPPING

Chop means to cut things into small pieces. The more you chop, the smaller the pieces. If a recipe says finely chopped, it means you need very small pieces.

CUTTING LENGTHWISE

To cut something lengthwise means to cut *along* its length. You create pieces that are the *same length* as they were initially.

SLICING

Slice means to cut something into thin pieces. Each slice should be about the same thickness.

CUTTING CROSSWISE

To cut something crosswise means to cut *across* its length. The pieces will be shorter, but the *same width* as they were initially.

TECHNIQUES

Tips for making great food art

MAKING FACES

Food art is all about creativity. The recipes in this book will get you started. But your imagination is really the secret ingredient! A recipe may call for black olives as the eyes. But why not try raisins instead? Use these techniques for inspiration. Add your personal style to create cool variations!

Eyes

GRAPE HALVES ON
MARSHMALLOWS

BLACK OLIVE SLICES
ON CREAM CHEESE

BLUEBERRIES ON
BANANA SLICES

BLACK OLIVES ON
HARD-BOILED EGGS

Noses

CANTALOUPE BALL

BABY CARROT

RAISIN

GRAPE TOMATO

Mouths

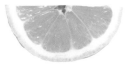

HALF A LEMON SLICE

RED PEPPER TOP

ORANGE SECTION

GREEN PEPPER SLICE

ATTACHING WITH GOOEY STUFF

Food art combines a variety of ingredients. How do you hold them all together? Ingredients such as cheese dip, pizza sauce, pasta sauce, and melted cheese can be used like glue. Plus, they taste great!

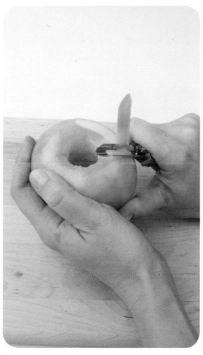

PREPARING APPLES

First, remove the apple core. Push the apple corer through the top of the apple near the stem. Make sure it goes all the way to the bottom. Then move the corer around the stem using a sawing motion. When you're done, you can simply pull out the core of the apple! Then peel the apple and cut it as directed in the recipe.

SEVERED FINGER
PIZZA

Can you give me a hand with dinner?

MAKES 1 PIZZA

INGREDIENTS

¼ cup pizza sauce

7-inch pizza crust

5 string cheese sticks

1 red bell pepper

2 tablespoons shredded cheddar cheese

2 tablespoons chopped black and green olives

TOOLS

measuring cups and spoons

spoon

cutting board

paring knife

baking sheet

1 Preheat the oven to 400 **degrees**. Spread the pizza sauce on the crust.

2 Cut each of the string cheese sticks in half. Arrange them on the pizza.

3 Core the red pepper, removing the seeds and stem. Cut out ten fingernail shapes. They should be as wide as the string cheese sticks. Put one at the end of each cheese stick.

4 Put the shredded cheese in the middle. Then add the chopped olives. Chop the rest of the pepper. Add 1 tablespoon of chopped red pepper to the pizza.

5 Place the pizza on a baking sheet. Bake for about 15 minutes.

15

FLOATING HEAD
CIDER

This spooky cider will make heads roll!

INGREDIENTS

1 cup lemon juice

1 tablespoon salt

4 large Granny Smith apples

16 raisins

2 gallons apple cider

TOOLS

measuring cups and spoons

mixing bowl

peeler

apple corer

paring knife

cutting board

paper towels

parchment paper

baking sheet

stew pot

1 Preheat the oven to 250 **degrees**. Mix the lemon juice and salt in a medium bowl. Peel the apples. Use the corer to remove the cores and seeds. Cut the apples in half lengthwise.

2 Carve a face into the round side of each apple half. Try giving them different **expressions**!

3 Put the apple faces in the lemon juice mixture for 1 minute. Then set them on a paper towel for a few minutes.

4 Cover the baking sheet with parchment paper. Put the apples face up on the baking sheet. Bake for about 90 minutes. The apples should be a little brown around the edges.

5 Remove the apples from the oven. Stick a raisin into each eye.

6 Pour the cider into the stew pot. Put the dried apple faces in the cider so they float face up. Serve it warm or cold.

TO DIE FOR
DIP

Nothing goes with cheesy dip like fingers and brains!

INGREDIENTS

5 carrots

1 cauliflower head

1 cup cheese dip

1 tablespoon salsa

5 almond slices

TOOLS

peeler

measuring cups
and spoons

bowl

toothpick

1 Peel the carrots. Break the cauliflower into large **florets**.

2 Put the cheese dip in a microwave-safe bowl. Microwave for 30 seconds. The cheese dip should be warm. Add a little more time if needed.

3 Add the salsa into the cheese dip. Use a toothpick to swirl the salsa into the cheese. Don't mix it completely.

4 Use a dab of cheese dip to stick the almond slices to the narrow end of each carrot.

5 Stick the carrots into the dip. Arrange them so they look like fingers on a hand!

6 Place the bowl on a serving plate. Arrange the cauliflower around the bowl.

EYEBALL
SPAGHETTI

Serve this creepy delight family style!

INGREDIENTS

1 bag frozen meatballs

16 ounces spaghetti noodles

16-ounce jar pasta sauce

2 string cheese sticks

about 10 green olives with pimiento

TOOLS

baking sheet

large pot

strainer

saucepan

wooden spoon

paring knife

cutting board

1 Place the meatballs on a baking sheet. Cook as directed on the package.

2 Boil the spaghetti noodles in a large pot. The box will tell you how long to cook them. When they are done, **strain** the noodles and set them aside.

3 Put the pasta sauce in a saucepan over medium heat. Stir until warm.

4 Add the noodles and stir. Keep the pasta warm until your meatballs are done.

5 Put some spaghetti on each plate. Arrange meatballs on top.

6 Slice the cheese sticks crosswise. Slice the olives. You'll need a slice of each for each meatball.

7 Place the slices of cheese and olive on the meatballs and serve.

GROSS-OUT
PITA

Look out! This pita ate too much cheese!

INGREDIENTS

1 small pita pocket

¼ cup shredded
mozzarella cheese

3 tablespoons pizza
sauce

½ cup shredded lettuce

1 grape tomato

1 slice mozzarella
cheese

1 black olive, sliced

1 red bell pepper

TOOLS

kitchen scissors

spoon

baking sheet

spatula

paring knife

cutting board

1 Preheat the oven to 350 **degrees**. Use kitchen scissors to cut an oval in the top of the pita.

2 Stuff the shredded cheese into the pita. Then spoon in the pizza sauce.

3 Put the pita on a baking sheet. Bake it for 15 minutes. While it's baking, put some lettuce on a plate.

4 Remove the pita from the oven. Put it on top of the lettuce.

5 Cut the grape tomato in half. Place one half above the hole in the pita. This is the nose.

6 Cut two circles of sliced cheese. Place them above the tomato. Put slices of black olive on top of the cheese slices. These are the eyes.

7 Place pieces of red pepper above the eyes. These are the eyebrows.

8 Use a spoon to pull some melted cheese and sauce out of the hole in the pita.

23

GARBAGE GOOP

There are sweet treats inside these garbage cans!

INGREDIENTS

1 package blue gelatin dessert mix

gummy worms

fruit leather roll

pull and peel licorice

gummy bugs

TOOLS

3 6-ounce clear jars

mixing bowl

spoon

ladle

1 Put the gummy worms, fruit leather strips, and licorice in the jars. Leave lots of loose ends hanging out.

2 Mix the **gelatin** according to the directions on the box. But don't let it cool.

3 Use a ladle to spoon equal amounts of the gelatin mixture into each jar.

4 Put the jars in the refrigerator for four hours.

5 Remove the jars from the refrigerator. Place the gummy bugs on top of the gelatin desserts.

BLOODY HAND
PUNCH

What happened to the missing finger?

INGREDIENTS

2 cups apple juice

2 cups cranberry juice

2 cups 7-Up

6 ounces raspberries

red food coloring

TOOLS

sterile rubber glove (the kind without powder inside)

measuring cups

round container with vertical sides

spoon

pitcher

punch bowl

1 Fill the rubber glove with water. Tie the wrist in a knot. Put the hand in the freezer for at least one day.

2 Remove the glove from the frozen hand. It's okay if a finger breaks off. That just makes it even creepier! You could save the finger to float in the punch.

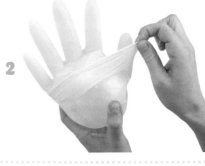

3 Put a few inches of water in the round container. Put the hand in the container so the fingers point up. Make sure the bottom of the hand is in the water. Put it in the freezer for several hours.

4 Mix the apple juice, cranberry juice, and 7-Up in a pitcher. Put the punch in the refrigerator. Wait until you are ready to serve the punch. Then fill the punch bowl half way.

5 Remove the hand from the round container. Set the hand in the punch bowl. Pour more punch into the bowl until it is full.

6 Rinse the raspberries and add them to the punch. Put drops of red food coloring on the hand to look like blood.

SNOT STICK
PRETZELS

Gross, gooey, and good!

INGREDIENTS

1 cup of cheese dip

2 or 3 drops of green food coloring

¼ cup shredded mozzarella cheese

1 tablespoon pickle relish

8 large pretzel sticks

TOOLS

measuring cups and spoons

small bowl

spoon

prep bowl

1 Put the cheese dip in a small bowl. Add the green food coloring. Put in one drop at a time. Stir between drops. Add drops until it's a nice, snotty green color!

2 Add the mozzarella cheese. Stir until well mixed.

3 Stir in the pickle relish.

4 Fill a prep bowl with some of the cheese mixture. Set it in the middle of a plate.

5 Break the pretzels in half. Dip the broken end of each pretzel stick into the remaining cheese mixture. Set the pretzels on the plate around the prep bowl.

WRAP IT UP!

Food art finale!

Now you're ready to **design** your own creepy food art! It helps to have a plan before you start. Make a **sketch** of your idea. Add notes about what ingredients will work best. Talk about your sketch with others. You will get great ideas! Make sure you get the camera out and take a photograph of your creation. The better your creepy foods look, the more likely they are to be eaten!

It's good to learn about food. The foods we eat have a lot to do with how we feel. The more familiar you are with the food around you, the better! Learning to make food teaches us about **nutrition** and health. Learning to make food art teaches us to have fun at the same time!

GLOSSARY

ALTERNATIVE – different from the original.

APPROXIMATION – about the right amount.

CANVAS – a type of thick cloth that artists paint on.

DEGREE – the unit used to measure temperature.

DESIGN – to plan how something will appear or work.

EXPRESSION – 1. creating a work of art as a way to show one's feelings. 2. the way someone's face looks that shows his or her feelings.

FLORET – a piece of broccoli or cauliflower that does not include the stem.

GELATIN – a powder used to make jelly and some desserts.

NUTRITION – how different foods affect one's health.

SKETCH – a drawing.

STRAIN – to remove the liquid from a mixture of solids and liquids.

Web Sites

To learn more about cool food art, visit ABDO Publishing Company on the World Wide Web at **www.abdopublishing.com.** Web sites about cool food art are featured on our Book Links page. These links are routinely monitored and updated to provide the most current information available.

INDEX

A

Adult help (for safety), 5, 6, 7
Apples (preparation of), 13
Attaching (of ingredients), 13

B

Beverages, 16–17, 26–27
Buying (of ingredients), 7

C

Candy (food art made with), 24–25
Cheese (food art made with), 14–15, 20–21, 22–23, 28–29
Cheese dip, 18–19, 28–29
Chopping, 11
Cider, 16–17
Cleanliness, 6
Clothing (while making food art), 6
Cooking terms, 11
Creativity (with food), 4, 6, 7, 12, 30
Cutting, 11

D

Desserts, 24–25
Dips, 18–19, 28–29
Drinks, 16–17, 26–27

F

Faces (creation of), 12, 16–17, 20–21, 22–23
Fruits
buying, 7
food art made with, 4, 7, 16–17, 26–27
washing, 6

G

Gelatin, 24–25

H

Hair (while making food art), 6
Hands (creation of), 18–19, 26–27

I

Ingredients, 8–9
buying, 7
measuring, 6
preparing, 5, 6, 30
storing, 7
types of, 4, 5, 8–9, 30
washing, 6

J

Juice (food art made with), 16–17, 26–27

K

Knives
safety with, 5, 6, 7
uses of, 11

M

Main dishes, 14–15, 20–21, 22–23
Measuring (of ingredients), 6
Meatballs (food art made with), 20–21

N

Nutrition, 30

O

Oven use, 5, 7

P

Pasta sauce (food art made with), 20–21
Permission (for kitchen use), 5
Photographs (of food art), 30
Pitas, 22–23
Pizza, 14–15

Pizza sauce (food art made with), 14–15, 22–23
Preparation (for making food art), 5, 6, 30
Pretzels, 28–29
Punch, 26–27

R

Recipe (reading of), 5

S

Safety, 5, 6, 7
Salsa (food art made with), 18–19
Sketches (of food art), 30
Slicing, 11
Snack foods, 18–19, 28–29
Soda (food art made with), 26–27
Spaghetti, 20–21
Storage (of ingredients), 7
Stove use, 5, 7

T

Techniques (for making food art), 12–13
Terms (about cooking), 11

Tools, 10
preparing, 5
safety with, 6
types of, 10
washing, 6

V

Vegetables
buying, 7
food art made with, 4, 7, 14–15, 18–19, 22–23
washing, 6

W

Washing (of hands, ingredients, and tools), 6